God had a body

BLUE LIGHT BOOKS

JENNIE MALBOEUF

God had a body

Poems

Indiana University Press
Indiana Review

This book is a publication of

Indiana University Press
Office of Scholarly Publishing
Herman B Wells Library 350
1320 East 10th Street
Bloomington, Indiana 47405 USA

iupress.indiana.edu

Manufactured in the United States of America

Library of Congress Cataloging-in-Publication Data

Names: Malboeuf, Jennie Maria, author.
Title: God had a body: poems / Jennie Maria Malboeuf.
Description: Bloomington, Indiana: Indiana University Press/
  Indiana Review, [2020] | Series: Blue Light Books.
Identifiers: LCCN 2019021139 (print) | LCCN
  2019021533 (ebook) | ISBN 9780253047267 (ebook)
  | ISBN 9780253047243 (pbk.: alk. paper)
Classification: LCC PS3613.A4326 (ebook) | LCC PS3613
  .A4326 A6 2020 (print) | DDC 811/.6—dc23
LC record available at https://lccn.loc.gov/2019021139

1 2 3 4 5 25 24 23 22 21 20

for David & Mavis

Concerning the condition of the sons of men, God tests them, that they may see that they themselves are *like* animals.

—Ecclesiastes 3:18

Contents

III

Acknowledgments

Thank you to

Verse Daily for reprinting "Parable";

Poetry Singles for featuring "Grandmothers";

Mary Szybist for anthologizing "Grandmothers" in *Best New Poets 2016* and Kyle Dargan for reprinting "The Men" in *Best New Poets 2018*;

the *Pushcart Prize Anthology* for listing "Hubris" as a Special Mention in 2019;

the Dorothy Sargent Rosenberg Prizes for awarding "Newfound Star System";

Dana Gioia for accepting "Ruth" for the *VQR*;

the North Carolina Arts Council for a 2019-2020 Fellowship

the presses who listed my manuscript or individual poems as finalists for publication or prizes, especially *PRISM* (Canada) and *Spoon River Poetry Review* (as well as G. C. Waldrep for judging their 2016 poetry prize);

the University of Virginia and Jeb Livingood for hosting (Matthew Wimberley and) me for a reading in February 2017;

my teachers, professors, classmates, and colleagues at the following institutions:

Holy Family Catholic School, especially Sister Rose Andrew and Sister Agnes Marie;

Centre College, especially Lisa Williams, Philip White, and
  Leslie Singleton;

the University of North Carolina at Greensboro, especially Fred
  Chappell, Stuart Dischell, Van Jordan, Julia Johnson, Terry Kennedy,
  and the late Jim Clark, as well as Jaimee Hills and Jennifer Whitaker;

Guilford College, especially Mylène Dressler and our visiting writer,
  Ada Limón;

the *Indiana Review* and Indiana University Press, especially Essence
  London, Hannah Kesling, and Adrian Matejka for awarding this
  prize and Ashley Runyon, Nancy Lightfoot, Megan Schindele, Rachel
  Rosolina, and Holly Hess for all their help in editing my book;

my family, especially Mama (Alice), Dad (F. Stephen), and my brother
  (George Thompson);

and, finally, to my dog Mavis, a divine creature and the greatest of the
  dozens of animal species I address here;

and, my husband, David, a miracle.

God had a body

The Godhead

When God had a Body,
He went on foot like an animal
through thick trees to spy on His creation.

While in said form, He looked cross
at the first two playing hide-and-seek
with their flesh in leaves and branches.

He revealed Himself in parts. Eye
and arm, ear, fist, face, angel wing, and feather.
                    Jacob beat God down.
How perfectly strange to know suffering
before it happened. A cipher:
at genesis, to know then is worse,

that the second would spill out
one son from her womb to kill the other,
that Your Own Body is a memory

of events that haven't yet happened—
a Son who is Your spitting image,
who knows the outcome coming for you.

Imagine God bathing with water and lye,
ash, sand, a handful of black soil.
Imagine God dressing, putting on a body
to blend in. Does one bathe a body

that one puts away? Does one sleep and eat
for it? *God has no body*, they say. God has
nobody.

I

First Death Ever Filmed

It isn't clear who was there,
because you don't watch them;
you see the elephant, the milk
and crackle of old film around her.
It's hard to make out how it happens,
but in seconds she falls stage right.
Chains on her legs.
Her tons no thing at all to electric
current. Her fingerlike trunk
with scars the shape of a cigar tip.
Topsy seems a joke name
now, but the same was done
before. In fact, after Big Mary   swung
and stomped that circus worker
for poking her sore tooth,
she was hoisted by a rail crane,
              neck   c r a c ked
from the weight of her body,
ears hanging like cold cuts,
tiny smile still plastered to her
clown face.

Christ is a Great Blue Heron

I saw Him today walking on the cold water;
He only appears when alone. This vision
was a horror. The clear lake, the distance.
He seems to be in oblivion. He is not.
His serene voice trills and chimes like the wind
through frozen feathers.
                He has been on either side
of the reservoir, where He watches and waits,
a figure to study, His nest unseen. In the Gospels,
Jesus was hungry and cornered by beasts.
The devil himself wanted stones turned to bread
and for Christ to fall, then fly with the angels.

Christ is a snake falling from a tree.
When I look down, He is there also.
A copperhead but only body. The pattern
puts a fear in my belly. Crossbands,
almost trinities time and again. Some snakes
hide well in red mud, your foot across
their backs before you see them wake. In the Incredulity
of Thomas, in front of the new apostle, even,
Jesus asks for his hand inside the open wound.

Christ is a fish; He is many. In Matthew,
there are men inside fish; there are fish
with coins in their heads.

The Cow's Eye

Daddy picked it up from the stockyards;
stringy and soft, the eye f l o a t e d.
                        Like the film lid
that comes natural to chicken grease and fat,
the jar we couldn't pour down the sink.
He said it'd help with my science project, a neat
counterpart to my plastic painted model kit.
Something real to show. The other kids
had dioramas or little tightly worked explosions.
Even the teachers and parents dodged and winced.
Two boys dared themselves to eat the eye, asked if
I'd pay to watch. But to me it was a perfect black circle,
so pretty I squinched hard and wished it back to the socket,
the lashes, the awful, dumb gaze.

Animals in the Bible

Last week, on the other side
of the world, half a zoo floated away
while the rest drowned—
white tigers loose and fighting
the only way they knew how.
Out there still missing are a bear,
hippo, and hyena. Men too.
I picture them swimming the sky
without gravity, like the hunting dog
and soon-dead rabbit of Urania's Mirror.
Most of the animals in the Bible
are violent; even God is a *raging fire*
while Hell is a *fire that never ends.*
Jesus is seen in the morning
on a star chart. And sometimes
a lion is the devil and then, later,
Jesus again. The story I saw showed
the tiger, so un-orange, with his vicious grin
frozen in death. The story called him a *beast.*

Frog Gig, 1983

At face value, they aren't that scary;
their eyes are wider than yours.
It's their movements:
      their fat dying bodies on the lawn,
   their disconnected legs ticking
         with unused reflex
           to a pinch of salt in the fridge.
My father brought them home by the dozen.
He linked legs to gig line and stretched the chain
across the plot. The big bulls watched you.
Sometimes they would lunge. Days after,
I'd dream of walking across the grass
to get to our garden, the ground grainier
than usual, cold and bellowing. I forgot
they camouflaged so well. Yards in, it hit me,
     and, too late
to turn around,
     the floor thick with ready grins.

Some Things Have Been Heard Enough

Most of what I remember was on a kitchen floor.
Daddy played his new cassette of country jokes;
we laughed because he laughed. In summertime,
he'd lay our heads against the plexiglass of the wood
table and use a box of Q-tips to clean our ears like gun barrels.
Daddy told a story about a pet rabbit hutch, but then
by the end they were cleaned too. This one time,
at the height of an anecdote, a mosquito, a female,
flew inside his head. She beat her wings
so hard he jumped from his chair. When Mama
drove him home from the doctor, he showed us
the mold of hot wax they poured to pull her—
preserved in flight—right out.

Grackles

Birds have made a nest
of our outbuilding—short work of it,
better use of it perhaps. Boat-tailed
or red-bellied. Mama would
call these *starlings*, as if they were
descendants of the stars, their children.
Little feathery babies. Changelings,
turning and growing things. I don't
know which name is a proper title
for them. One sounds crisp,
the other darling. Anytime
I'd spot some purplish fowl, she used to
tell that story once more of the man
who lived next door to her childhood
home: long rope tied to his dogwood
tree. He'd wait for starlings to roost
by the dozens and then jerk his string and cackle,
watching the branches explode.
Remember? she'd say. Just as though,
on the face of it, an eggling, I was there.

Wilding

I should be able to recall
the reason I was touching
that cat. Daddy asked why
I did it. He told me not to.
I do remember where I was:
the little corner when the house
forms an *L*, before the addition
walked you to the outbuilding,
before the bedroom of our cousins'
country house had caught fire—a dry pump
and bucket on one side and gravel lot
on the other. I always had a skirt on,
so most likely I had a skirt on then.
I squatted down, I know that,
held out my hand for her.
Thought I could gentle her fur.
She broke the skin; I tried to cry soft.
She looked full of kittens. Daddy said
we'd have to wait a couple weeks
to watch if she turned up dead.
To make sure I didn't catch something bad.

Ruth

The whale washed ashore. Its still
body lay for days—turning and turning
one new color after another. White,
then gray, black, then a sort of white
again. The water barely skimmed
its bottom lip, mouth hung open
like a friendly doorway. The townies
took pictures inside its head, captioned
Jonah! with a cursory smile and dot eyes
in their scrapbooks. The flesh started
to funk, smelling beyond the boardwalk,
that certain scent of ending. By then,
the townies had stopped with the visits,
their cameras, the peeking over
the brushy hills to check if it remained.
A few fishermen thought to *push the fish
back in*, let its husk—little house—disappear
into the mouths of thousands of other fish.
But their boats weren't big enough, and the nets
that tangled the whale to begin with were wasted.
The job required hours of digging, big trucks,
gravity. What was the whale rolled on its back,
and they covered the belly with dirt.

Sacred Heart

Sometimes the Bible repeats
Itself. Abraham like God and
Isaac like Jesus. Abraham, knife
in hand, sobbing but ready.

Sometimes we add to it. Fish
spreading like wildfire in the sea,
on loaves of bread. Teresa
with the little baby heads floating

around her in my book of saints.
Cecilia at the piano, even the same
in death. Gorgeous with blush
just run from her cheeks. Mary's heart

       b u r s t s into gold
on my faded green statue. What
to do with these images as little
children. Marvel at their mystery,

the magic: necessity is the mother
of invention, they say.

Animals

The parakeet I gave up
                 to the couple next door
          found his way
                              to a wet truck
in the alley. It was an odd sight.
Too blue and yellow, he seemed electric.
My brother scooped him in an old shirt, and his eyes,
still blank, somehow trembled. Within hours, the bird
was taut and closed on the floor of the cage.
I can't keep him, I told my mother. *He ate his babies.*

When I first took him home in a paper takeout box,
he chirped and chirped. He sang so much I knew
I could make him talk. Each night I played
a tape of short phrases for him to learn:
hello, friend, and *thank you*. But he didn't work like a parrot.

He only brushed himself against my girl-bird's chest,
panting and flapping hotly. And one day I caught him—
he sat heavy on their rubber chicken of a chick,
little downy feathers smooshed, with the same stare.

The Meaning of God

A plain-bellied snake waits near the bridge
in the park. Her body is gray and heavy.
Her skin looks to feel of hard fruit

packed with sand. For two days, her body
moves like a nightmare: once quick
swim into the lake, once shifts so small

I think my mind is full of tricks. *Creeping
things* against *the vault of the sky.*
Above, large birds stomp their dead babies

back into the nest. Their dead babies
become the nest.
                  The birds we kept
in cages fought any mirror;
God & animal, God versus image,
                            God versus God.

A Figure for the Holy Ghost

When my body was small,
I was taught not to borrow
trouble. Learned the sign
of the cross: forehead to belly,
left shoulder to right. Made
cocked *X*s in mosquito bites
and smacked the sting away.

The Spirit held His body up.
The plank of tree trunk
where Christ's hands were
nailed. The whole of His weight
hanging on that beam.
The Spirit can do anything.
The Spirit, like Atlas. The Omega.

Signified with water, alongside
fire. Signified with a bird,
with the air itself. The Spirit
will speak up for you
when your mouth is dry.
When you can't force
the words out, like a loud

father, the Spirit will take
the mic. Years later,
the Spirit moves through
you like liquor. *It was the Spirit
speaking,* you say. The Spirit
in bed with someone. A genius
Cyrano. Courage.

The Spirit is a guide into
the wild forest. A baby
leaping inside. The semen

scattered to start
the baby to begin with.
A gift, a threat. Something
one can never speak

against. The source. The voice
changing. The sun is merely all
the colors you can see.

II

The Country

The fish had babies
in her belly. Daddy spilt
them out on the picnic
table by accident, I guess.
He slit her body from
tip to tang: Velcro lips
and a shiny vinyl tail. *Those are her*
eggs, he said. Pretty bubbles.
Her skin a sequin gown.
Empty eyes black as the city sky.

Orrery

Cassiopeia sits opposite the Big Dipper,
which makes sense. One is a vessel
and the other empty, or
one is an empty
vessel and the other isn't there.
One is a plough and the other
a winsome woman.
We lie on our backs and
flatten the grass like circling
dogs. Dark sky objects.
Through the shitty telescope,
we see Saturn, we think. I like
the life we live but hate life. Or
I love life but hate the life I live.
Most orbits are not perfect circles.
And the constellations are shaped
like dogs.

The Leonids

On the best of days, I hear
that guy who called me
sultry at a party three years ago
while 10cc played, heady and strange,
on the radio.
        On the worst, I think of
the year I lost my virginity:
I watched the stars like sperm
and read Charles Wright nonstop.
I sported lip gloss with a pink sheen
and a blue toboggan with a white ball
on top. The world was exploding.
All the while, I let this boy lay beside
me in a cow field in Kentucky.
For seconds between star shots,
I closed my eyes (filling with wet
Milky Way glaze).
        In November, I saw hundreds
of meteorites. In December, the ground
was ticking with the bodies of living birds.

Early Signs of the Apocalypse

The barking became unbearable.
And my dog, wholly ready most days,
didn't bother to join in. She nudged
and pawed me out of bed *so late,*
staring wide-eyed at my ignorance.
It's only noon, I cussed, *and my day off.*

From what? she turned her head.
She meant, *What are we waiting on?*
In truth, I dreamt of my exes all crossing
paths (which surely will happen soon enough),
and, for the sixth time this season,
beat my father almost to death.

Zoonosis

Cat in the briar behind the house.
I bark her away, crouch
down to her level with the dog.
Cat licks can blind, I read.
Their cries the whistle of the devil,
teeth working like scissors. When she finally
untangles herself, finds her way to her own
porch, the dog squeals with joy.
She'll be back, I warn. Each day we find
more kittens, orange and black,
tiny faces amounting to only open eyes:
a destruction.

Song of the Cock

In the dark, the ortolan eats
and eats. He is a dumb bird.
Easily tricked, his appetite

is used against him. If just
the tiniest speck of light
were to hit his face, he might

say *when*. As is, his bite
is relentless. Like the night
I watched a goat finish

tire after tire before retiring
unfulfilled. He found himself
          at a great height—

little hooves held tight
against the quarry wall.
This bunting bird, though,

he is a different type of secret:
we must hide during the meal.
What to do to this fat body

in a modest pot, golden belly and slight
feet? My mother covered up
in the same way, late

for Mass, a makeshift napkin veil
for all the girls.

Men in My Bed as Dead Animal in Dog Mouth

Almost as proof to herself she could
catch it and surprise us along with her,
daring to let it loose half alive in the house

or carry it forever inside her head,
the dog scratches the back door
with her paw, limp rabbit doll held

tight in her teeth. This isn't the first
kill. Not the only mistake she's made.
She rolled around in the spot

where the rock dove transformed into
a paperweight. If the need
weren't so basic. The stalking, the bait,

control of another's reflex, his body's
final pulses against the soft palate of a cave,
a river.

Original Meal

It was an unfair game, temptation.
Eden sowed tight with juicy foods,
each redder than the tips
of the heavy branch just before.
And how tricky to be told
that biting could lead to knowing
and that knowing all could kill you.
With only two people, such hearsay.
What was it He said? *Mali.* Possession.
Adam's throat blocked by apple, bread
of life, the flesh of his own children,
yet to be born:
unable to denounce, unable to swallow.
Lips, teeth, tongue, neck, body, body, body.
One aware that one fruit will end them.
The second thinking she'd found a way.

Landscape Where I Forget My Father

The four corners of my eyeline are rich with distraction.
An aquarium, a library, a fun park, a creek. In this scene,
a shrike crosses the sky, spears a frog on some barb for later.

He looks like a songbird but is known as a butcher. In the map center
is a half acre with dead dogwoods, a blue spruce, a fence built flush
with another fence. The dogwood trees are so dried out that they fall

from just a push.

Blindfold

There is life you cannot see
with your hands: cottonmouth,
barred owls, an unbroken horse.
In truth, you have closed your eyes
before to look at your crush's dark braids,
to picture her better. By yourself,
she visits you when your face is shut,
trapping observation beneath hair,
skull, and skin.
                    Now, you attempt
                to move past her
without bumping her breasts against
                    your rough elbow again.

To you, this is no party game.
You think, *Why am I always sightless,*
bound, covered up, and handed
a weapon to work with? For a moment,
you forget what is being played.
Is there a sharp tail or a stick
in your right hand?
                    You might pin the tail
            on yourself or take a swing
                    at the invisible piñata,
                which rustles like a woman's hair

and exists only in your ear—inside
the small, wrapped box of imagination.
In sunlight, her black hair shows
itself as heat.
                    You can feel this—
her head radiates
                a grained energy
            as your left hand wanders her neck.

She giggles as you trip
            over her small feet,
        and you recall the sound

of turkeys from an abandoned farm
            years ago. There, you learned
                how to identify animals,
            repeating their names in your mind
            each time one appeared.
                Here, to help,
            she pushes you away,
        guides you toward
                what everyone else
already sees.

The Waxwing

moves his food
through a game
of telephone. He nips
a bit of fruit and hands
it off to the next bird
and that bird to another,

when eventually the last
waxwing eats it. Their sweet
stone becomes an heirloom,
willed time and again
to whoever accepts
and refuses to pass it on.

With other animals,
sometimes a father offers
a way out. A warning.
His assistance fragile.
A set of fins or superlimbs
that soften and dissolve   against the sun.

A candle rather
than plumage,
consumed into shine.

This absurd push
a murder really.
Wings made of grease
          from the bellies of bees.
Who on earth
would do that
to their child?

The waxwing is a lovebird.
He noses and grooms.

Apricot-breasted, his tail is silky;
he hides his eyes
with a black mask.
He sports a tiny blood

drip on the tip
of his lift feathers.
Six on a side, a spare
appendage.

Animals in Captivity

A zoo in a river town.
On cold nights, the people
could hear the lion. The lion
wanted to be known in the dark.
His roar: a body opening
by force. Claws cracking
a breastbone and tearing away
the skin. A demon choir.
Some nights the lion was loose
in the park and the gates on lockdown.
The people wondered what the lion
might eat first if he wandered away.
When not speaking, the folds
in the human throat
spread out like a vagina.
The vagina tender as a mouth.
A moan a confused sort of canticle.
        The lion's call was an earworm
in deep sleep. The dream the people
have where they forget what
they are running from. Or where
a monster stands at the ends of their beds,
and in waking life they cannot move
their limbs. Where they scream disbelief
into an animal mouth at why God created evil
to begin with.

The Nightjar

eats like a bat. She flies,
mouth open, swallowing
whole her fellow birds:
wrens and warblers.
Locusts and moths.
On both sides of her
toad face is a bristly
mustache. She hides
in bracken fronds, among
fiddleheads. She nests right
there on the ground. If not
for her song, the nightjar
might be unknown. Her feathers
are leaves, her body mistaken
for brush. A watchful eye,
a nothing, a banshee.

phylum::class::order::family::genus

              mother
loved   them   so   much
when we were children:
their ruby throats,   not
necks, which must've
held p r e c i o u s stones
inside. Mama was quiet
too. Daddy says I *should've*
    been a nun. Mama kept us
fed with fat bugs and worms.
She made a tiny bed
of sticks and strings.
A skirt of velvet with an elastic
waist, a spool of thread
from spider silk.
The hummingbird's wings
don't always move but look
      like
      they
      do. Mama never
sat for dinner, never slept.

The Giving Away

I woke up angry.
The headless snake found
by the apple trees dried
and shrunk on the steps.
Though he was small as
an earthworm yesterday,
I relished seeing him dead.
And without his teeth, his eyes,
his tongue, his tiny non-ears,
even then his slick-scurry land-swim
didn't have much weight.
He thought he knew something,
I bet. Had something over me.

Repletion

The moon is confused. He wears a pointy crown
tonight like the sun. And the nightly news said the ocean
is *too salty*. The waters are thick with sharks.
I had the dumb idea of going to the beach once more.
By then, half a dozen kids had lost their limbs.
The headline: *Men Catch Shark in Kill Devil Hills.*
As if the animal was to blame.
Today the clocks were reset in London—
an extra moment tendered—and I thought about
that slumber party during Lent when
we ordered pizza with meat ground into the sauce.
How my friend's mother thought we should wait
until midnight to eat it, a Saturday. The last time I spoke
to that girl was years after, high school already. She recounted
a story of swimming with a strange guy from work,
his later coming on her back, and laughed while I listened in horror.
I pictured the little porcelain southern belle statues across her
bookshelves, each with a golden year number to represent
growing up; us practicing country falsetto; sneaking a dirty movie
on the basement TV, not knowing what it was we were seeing—
sweetly stupid, legs dangling limp over the couch.

Snake-handling

Daddy carried them in both hands—
whipping and
       curling
   violently. He walked past me,
arms stretched out   center
as if he were holding a screaming baby.
He dropped them, wholly tails, in a tall white bucket
where they shifted
     just   enough
to prove they were more than rope.
They stopped short, he said.

He had hit newborn rabbits
before by mistake, some of them leaping
free like fireworks from the dull blade.

Fear

This morning opened up
like a long fall from the sun.
That snake we found coiled
under trash bags in the yard
was patient while being discovered.
For some reason, you threw him clear.
Midflight, he danced as the ribbon
moves from an Olympic gymnast's wrists:
flicked spastic and out of place.
His green-black body painted a rainbow
across—what seemed—an acreage of sky.

What the Eclipse Does to Animals

Right when I left home, the sky went dark.
Not where I could see it. But the whole kingdom
of animals confused on the almost-other side of the world.

I spent my first year away unsettled. By May,
my wet hair parted like a lightning strike.
Outside this house, a mockingbird cries

under the streetlamp, pleading for company.
The false light keeps him awake, makes him
stupid. Just last night, in Spain, a crowd of fairgoers

lit a bull's horns and then loosened his chain.
They clapped and laughed when he rammed
into his own post, skull smashed but still afire.

Back then, I thought I was dying. It was the end
of hope. Panic set in to lose my virginity. This time
around, you and I plan a trip to the zoo. The moon

should pass right between us and the sun. Shadow
and starshine shaping an hourglass, the elephants
and ostriches become nocturnal, the entire menagerie

a mirror image of itself.

The Miracle of the Pigs

There are animals that kill themselves.
Most often they leap from great heights,
knowing full well what might happen.
Ten years back, in the Alps, two dozen
cows fell into a valley of rocks. Not all
at once, but one by one, over the course
of three days. The first went down,
and the others, like little sheep, followed.
The townspeople guessed
them thunderstruck or spooked
by larger threats. Tame, they belonged
to a farmer, noted by the bells around
their necks.   Because nothing
could reach them, their bodies
were lifted by helicopter, for fear
their passing would poison the nearby
springs.

In Matthew, two men or one man
that was many, a demoniac, pleaded
with Jesus not to rid them *before the time.*
To put their madness into the pigs.
And at once, the one man that was many
was back in his *right mind.* The two
thousand pigs drowned   themselves
in the water below.   In Matthew,
the townspeople want Jesus to leave. *Abyss*
means without depth. *Gorge* means the valley,
the throat, to eat oneself to death.

Landscape Where I Miss My Mother

In it is the moon, for certain.
A rabbit distracting advancing foxes
from her young. A wren amusing me
in the same way. There would be a river
because there was one. A nearby haunted zoo
where, every fall, a horseman chased a small train
down a hill.

      I cannot think of my mother without
thinking of myself. This is the true test:
she made herself a shadow, tiny prey.
Somewhere in the line of the almost
too-distant, where the scene looks deep
but flat and fake, soft mountains behind
the sharp sublime, a house. Puffs of smoke
from the working chimney. A picnic table
crowded with nightshades and stone fruit.
A load of hand-sewn laundry hung out to dry
and forgotten.

Phobia, 1985

I was in the wayback
of our Chevy wagon,
with Mama and Daddy up front.
        In the corner, a cricket
    crossed his legs,
            tiny claves, guitar strings.
He was fast and excited.
I held my tongue as long as I could.
Daddy jerked the car over and swept
him out with a rolled-up paper,
then swatted me with it too.
Don't squeal, he said. *You scared us all.*

lullaby

a way to understand my father, you
say, is to see him as a child. okay:
he tells me he carried his bottle
by the tit until the milk ran dry.
that cousin Lucy, fur-trimmed hat
and coat, took it from his hand
nearly. he dropped it behind
some rocks just yards from home,
never to hold it again. he used to
sleep with it, better companion than   hurdling sheep,
but cried that first night alone while
his tears became a honeyed cream and its froth and fizz
the sweetest dream.

Grandmothers

Where does it all begin?
God is good; woman bleeds.
It was the Depression or before.
You were cooking over an open
greasy fire, and the house burned
to the ground. And you were cutting
the heads off chickens and laughing
at the horror of them walking backward
and dancing. And you were slitting
the throats of two-hundred-pound hogs.
And keeping your future husband
from priesthood with seven children.
You showed me my stuffed puppy,
legs in the air. *He's dead!* you said.
Or you were a little girl with an iron
and a board for Christmas. You learned
to drive stick in a field. And you gave
birth to Father jumping off trains,
or you gave birth to Mother,
who only gave birth to two.
You were a witch, our house
adorned with dead animals,
fish curling to free themselves
from the wall.

The Men

are calling again.
The men look through my purse.
The men follow me home,
block after block of treelined
streets from the library or the bar,
cussing *cunt cunt cunt*
a few steps behind.
The men hand me green apples,
saying *they're sweet; you're sweet.*
The men tell me they know me.
That they could sleep better
if I'd *just lay beside* them
in the tiny bed. They hurl the word
independent like an insult.
The men feed me evenings.
Worry. Warm beer to the side
of my mouth. One compliment.
The men ask me if I can *conjugate* amo.
They invite friends over
and put their arm around her,
my hand between their legs.
The men stop calling because my being
Catholic is *too much.* The gold-trimmed
cards of Mary watch them from the wall.
The men boast how they like us fat,
skinny, thick, short, blond-haired, black.
The men get mad when I teach myself to come
to what makes me jealous, when I ask
them to tell me what happens in the movies
they watch, when I can't come to
anything but the fantasies they have.

In the Myths

everyone was raped.
even the birds raped
women; the ocean too.
there was no undoing.
this was explanation:
fact of life. the hero,
as in Janus, was two-faced
and raped other nymphs
than the ones he saved.
in Rome, he was the *god*
of doors and beginnings,
and his accuser allayed
with *goddess of the hinge*.
hinge from *hang*. or almost
zipper in Italian.
the moral is trust no one.
the moral is gods take
what they want. the moral
is take heart: we are made
from this raping in their image.
or they in ours.

Kingdom

In Botswana, the lioness shape-shifts
into a lion. Most likely because
she can't carry her own babies, she drops
her scent over and over, climbs atop
the other lionesses in mock sex, kills
the cubs of her neighbors. The lioness
learns to roar and grows a beard-mane
like her larger counterpart. She passes
herself off for a true lion. Of all the land
predators, she could be the apex.
      In the sea, the game is the same:
the shy moon wrasse plays kittenish
at first. She buries her head in the sandy
floor to sleep or hide. But if need be,
she becomes louder, turns her green to blue,
collects his own eggs to eat, his own stash
of pretty girl fish.

Hubris

In the paper today, they say,
Damaged manhood causes school shootings.
All summer, every evening,
a swarm of bats circles
the bell tower down the street.
They squeal in delight, mouths

full with bottle flies and mosquitoes.
Gore nursing blood. Lucifer
was said to crow over injury.
His name means *light.* Or *Venus.*
Or *star.* Or *zodiac sign.* Hell
can mean *hidden* or *separate.*

Picture a young boy: perfect
in His Image as we all are,
his wings shook out tight
like filmy skin, a featherless
see-through cloak, standing
like a man for the first time—

his foot on the throat of who
made him.

The Women

Birds are carrying the snakes in this time.
How else did this one die half-curled on our step
covered in ants by dawn? The birds leave presents for us.
Little wormy snake, regret.   The women I knew married
young. Before they could drink, call the right cuts of
beef loud enough for the butcher to hear.
Prime from primal, round and plate and tenderloin.
The first child came in a year or two, sometimes early.
Giant sea bird dropping babies from a bindle.

Parable

God as a mother:
         He raises us
until we're ready and then

lets us alone. Or He warns us to shy away,
to run from His house. Or once while
He's washing dishes after another fight;

we, only twelve years old at the time,
threaten that we're *leaving as soon as*
we *turn eighteen.* We're *outofhere,* we say—

the words all scrunched together like
one big smack in His face. Even though
it wasn't His fault. When He dies, we mourn

Him. We worry with where to toss the ashes,
argue about where the ashes are inside
the house, roll our eyes that our sister

certainly lost them. We planned to make
amulets or charms and slide them down
chains that rest above our hearts or on our chests

at least. Now and again, our minds wander.
We muse at how we exited His Body. His belly
made into a cat's mouth. Naval/nose. Dimpled scar

a philtrum overtop a split lip. Our faces hangdog,
our names the first survivors on His death notice.

First Mirror

Before the looking glass, before amenity,
the calm water pitch black. Stock-still,
placid, undisturbed. Incident light beat
a filmy facade. How long a glance
did it take until eyes knew: eyes, nose, mouth?
Eve alone and confused. Reaching for the woman
caught in endless drowning. How long
until Adam joined his wife at the lake's edge?
Until she understood her own looks by matching
another's?
       Mirrors at some point were made of stone.
Icy and lambent. Smoke. Hard sand, soda, and lime.
Make believe a magpie accepts her own image.
Head turning in the likeness in smack perfect
time. What does it mean to see the self
and have the self stare back? The mind a hall of mirrors,
a mother (behind you) wishing your *hair had stayed black.*

The Screwworm

seeks out an open wound
or makes one
        where it wasn't   before.
She lays a clutch of eggs   and grasps
the tissue tightly with   toothy thorns.

Most often, she shoots for the nostril,
ear canal, eye, or asshole. If not
on hand, a baby's naval will do.
In the fall, deer the size of large dogs
hunt for bedmates to make more deer.

        This year, in the Keys,
one's brain is busied with the screwworm.
Teeming, chockablock, brimful with her.
She will gaslight him. She will live inside
the deer until he dies.

Mnemonics

For days on end we find paper money
where we walk the dog near the high school.
One dollar, five, strewn across the lot.
And then, two butterfly wings dropped a foot apart
from one another. As if, when left too close,
they'd mend and lift away. You remind me
to stop placing so much meaning on things.
Not everything is a sign, you said once. *Stop
reading the horoscopes,* you said yesterday.
I think of my mother's huge wall hanging,
composed entirely of dried wings. How it roused
some disruption inside of me when she
brought it home.   A landscape
shaped from taxidermied onion skins and stained glass.
A church made of bones. In the last turn, we hear
the buzz of a dragonfly like an old bulb in a hedge,
short-circuiting, electric, alive.

Ode to the Cannibal

The redback spider throws himself
into the hollow fangs of his beloved.
A little gymnast, he leaps midthrust.
Beforehand, he plucks the silky strings
of her web. Romances his darling.
Imagines himself as tremendous as her
body.
        The females are wholly themselves.
Bellies stuffed with the same. Their insides
spilling with their insides. Fat and happy.
Taking everything their sweethearts have
to give.
        Domestic hogs sometimes
savage their young. Feed on the babies
while the babies feed on them. Out of
necessity, mostly. Not enough
to go around. And there are the sea squirts,
who station their backs against rocks
and eat their own minds. The sea squirts
reclaim their parts, salvage a form,
house both genders, move water
through stigmata, start to glow
as they become who they are.

Man, Beast, Lion, Bird

. . . the first angel who sinned is called not a Seraph but a Cherub.
—Saint Thomas Aquinas

Of course you came in four minds.
It is nearly impossible to think about one
thing at a time these days. The wild parts of you
are so regal, the beast broken and tame. You move
like anxiety, an ever-open eye. In order
to protect, you must at once keep watch
on the present, the past, what happens next.
And, above all, the godawful.

How is it
that you were both the snake in the tree
and the tree's guard when life just began?
Wherever G_d is, you follow.
Being made perfect spoiled you like false fruit:
your skin parched as a reptile's, sweet-smelling
and tart as a quince.

God-man

Ultimately, all roads lead to God.
Even the thoughts about His absence
are thoughts about where He might be
or what monuments to put in His place.
Once that sculpture starts to ruin, lichen
eating through stone, the townsfolk rope
the waist or neck and use gravity against itself.
The plant crawling inside bringing the outcrop
to life. A blight.
The roads and thoughts are the same—the maze
a hedge garden. Bushes neatly trimmed and angular:
airtight syllogism. Known by rote. So if the question is the worst
(what is wicked? or why?), the answer will be God. An inevitability,
                                             an endpoint.
Carve out the minor premise, the years the sculpture
stood ignored. Forgotten. Without protest.
The midway spot where folk stop on the road
for water, to sleep, to check the map.
              God is a rock.
              All rock may dissolve.
              God will yield.
If the question is man, the answer God.
The body a goat, the head and heart of man.
If the animal man, the mind his God.
Angels dancing on the head of a pin.
The body a bird, or plumed wings on a man.
Inside a devil, evil. Within good, God.

Inscape

What I remembered yesterday was wrong.
A pile of snow is only a half-dead deer.
Not halfway dead but half a body.
Then we find one antler in the clearing:
the part we never walked toward. Later, I'll recall
my skirt as double-knit green, not the fake denim
I wear every day, which is most likely. I will lose
that it's April, and I sat outside in the wind
with my students while my hair tangled,
and I couldn't hear their comments
over the sound of mowing and trucks
on the closest road, but I pretended
and nodded at each idea. I will forget
you wore that ugly brown toboggan
the woman we both kind of hate made,
even though it's already spring.
That I thought, while we walked, that
maybe I'd learn more about what's coming
from a palm reader than a therapist.
Antler means *horn before the eye.*
Animals ago, the fangs of deer
                    shifted from their mouths
            to their brow.
I went back today, bone picking for the other antler,
the hope that when we start to fall apart,
it all goes at once. Our thoughts skeletons. Our heads
embarrassingly light and bald and ready to be new again.
The velvet peeling from great branch crowns leaving
just dead pink bone flowers.

Thought Inventory with Rorschach and Caesura

The first of the blots   two piglets kissing a bell.
Second: a bear cub   in love with his own image.
Blood rising like   clouds of troubling ideas—
a pulse keeping   count on my eardrum.
Then, two, always   two, women tied together
breathing with the same lungs, cut at each of their waists
to mimic the Black Dahlia. Brains upside down, stems
reaching out   as countries in a cold war
unspoiled islands full   of smaller egrets. Four cards in,
penguins, of course, a cobra   a skull in the style of O'Keeffe,
half cleft-mind, half vagina. Parts sharp-toothed serpent & delicate orchid.
Logic versus imagination.   The watercolors have started to wring
away again. By five, the obvious   trick—a bat or a monarch?
Some poisonous liar or   what consumes poison wholly itself.
And six is sickening.   A housecat as a skin rug?
Two sassy rabbits mating or   giving birth. Both certain she knows
the way. Finally, a dream of heaven   sherbet-ladder nirvana
for nutria, foxes, catamounts.   Fire to ice. Hellraiser
with antlers and smile.   Eyeless pit viper with tongue
that sees and catches scent. The last frame is balance, I expect. Every color
and organ, the spine, nothing, pieces of paper and paint. Dye and water.

Letting Go

There was a time I thought
I could handle it. We walked the hounds
around the neighborhood. They pulled
and bayed at any quarry. I asked Daddy
for the leash, or he just handed it over.
I was supposed to stand still
until he took it back,
but she started to jerk me down
into the ditch, and I let loose.
Daddy called her Patches
because she was pied.
She's the smart one, he said.
The girl dog tracked scent.
Her bay opened a throat of glass
and smoke. *Quarry* comes from
heart to be cleaned.

Topography of a Bird

The bird begins with a crown
and ends with a start, which really
is his tail. The bird has a whisker,
a shoulder, an ear patch, a neck.
The lore is not a story but the face
between eye and beak.
                       Within
the body is almost a mirror image:
left side as right side, spare
lung and lobe. In his throat,
a crop; in the crop, food.
In his throat, a box; in the box,
a song.

III

Newfound Star System

Let's not leave it.
We spent this morning with
your head between my legs,
and this afternoon I questioned
why we'd ever do anything else.
We held hands in the art museum
and laughed at the pocketless
pool table, the broom held by a balloon.
Without irony, you whispered, *I'm proud
of you*, tore down the rotting carport
to see the supermoon. I know I'm not
supposed to say, but I dreamt of kissing
my grade-school crush, him now blond
and six foot two, but knew—you know
how it's more about what you feel during?—
that I needed to marry you. That made his
long-awaited kisses stupid darts.

Double Star—

The circle of white dots
we look at isn't impressive.
I admit expecting more.
I mean, what we see with
our own eyes is larger.
Above the chatter of schoolgirls,
our guide says, *This is Andromeda*,
an entire colony of stars,
something we couldn't
get to without this scope.
The sun will die in five billion
years, he tells us. Over there
a dust spot lingers, a little light
left behind. You are the only person
on the planet who understands.
One thousand Earths fit inside
Jupiter, one thousand Jupiters
inside the sun.

Orbs

Even if the whole world goes to smash, God can make another world.
—Martin Luther

Made new, I would ask for most things the same.
Odd creatures: the peahen taken with the best
spotted suitor. The albino peacock here only
to show us how blue and green are merely excess gifts.
              That there are endless answers
to our questions of beauty. The pygmy owl
displays fake eyes on the back of his head,
a skull illusion. If not two-faced,
little pests might peck his real eyes,
or what's larger could kill him. Instead,
he dodges cats and eats the brains
of perching birds.
            How to get to this earth again,
each nicety a redo.

The Godwit

B i r d
body flying for days on end,

shifting sleep from one side
of the mind to the other,

like tossing and turning
on a pillow nonstop.

Dreams of flight
are the ones we can control.

My husband has them often,
his whole figure a kick.

These are his dreams in color,
in the hallway of his schoolhouse,

his mother standing in shadow,
still before him. An omen.

Once, in the dead of night,
he tapped the bedroom window,

smiled crazily to let him back in.
It was a terror: half a brain in use,

he could have killed me in our sleep.
Like the man in Canada who drove

the small hours in crosstown traffic,
climbed a flight of stairs to hack his in-laws

to death. *Wit* means creature; *God* is good.

To Begin With

It was a red-letter day.
We hiked a new path
just to see how long
it'd take us. Every fifteen
minutes or so, you loop
small laps, infinite eights,
backpedaling just to catch me
up. A husband now, you are
still full of surprises.
Nine years and seven miles in,
I'm told that your favorite dog
died under the mud porch
of your childhood home,
tucked himself into a tight hole
and was lost for days before
you all knew: the stink thick like hot
garbage through summer. And then
one day, his death assumed,
almost forgotten, your new dog
carried his skull out from a pile of bones.

Heavy Animals, or Frustrated Attempts to See God

        As a girl, I used to stare fiercely enough at the Eucharist
that I thought I saw a golden beam pierce the ceiling tiles
to reach the big host in the priest's hands.
        Here lately, our trips to the observatory have yielded
measly results. Their telescopes are no better than a magnifying glass.
The icy dust is *star-forming nebulae,* they say. *We are witnessing
conception* light-years away.

Immolation

The first God we knew was violent.
He fought with His own inventions.
First, He molded men from mud;
then, if they stood out of plumb,
He mashed them. The men were lit
and could run themselves. But
sometimes they needed things.
God was too smart,
so they nipped and bit
for His attention. The men
made excuses for Him. They passed
the time. They told stories. One about
a pelican and her chicks: what a sweet offering
she is, gouging her own breast to shower
her babies in blood. After she had killed
them, still just wide, stupid mouths
in her nest, she let her heart spill
like a waterfall. Their dart tongues
drinking as vampires. Her beak red
as the devil, sleeping head in her chest,
belching extra fish out her throat pouch,
all this resurrection mistaken for generosity.

The Hydra

In a perfect world, live forever.
As a penis-shaped creature with a spider
topping its head: a true horror. Cartwheel
and bud yourself further and further. Trees
on top of trees that break away softly,
like the hairs of dandelion clocks.
Mouth hole torn for each little meal,
then a tidy, secret healed wound.
In the myths, Hercules bested monster

after monster. The freshwater Hydra
he couldn't kill alone. When he cut
one snake head, a friend zipped the neck-body
with fire until the head of all heads was smote
under stone. This was the price Hercules
paid for being born. Half mortal,
half god, wholly unwanted. Would you want
to be everlasting? A never-ending body. Battles
eternal. The next beast, like the last, determined

to end you. To send you to an afterlife.

Eschatology

      Today was the last
      supermoon until
      I cannot bear
children. You saw a cat,
then hours later the same
cat dead in the street.
I watched a hawk splay
his wings like shoulders
hunched in victory over
his prey. It was a gloat
stance. His beak almost
blue. He was there, then
not there.
      Twilight and the yard is thick
with rabbits, housecats, stray dogs
in the alley. The killing frost chokes
out fireflies and mosquitoes.
      Animals that tell
time better than we do.
On the drive home, the moon
followed me like the eyes
of a Jesus painting. The pink-
orange ring-beam unreal.
The white punched edge
of the moon like confetti.

The Gospels

In Psalms, we are made
of *wonder* and *fear*. In the Gospels,
the story is told over and again
from different points of view.
Evidence is collected: more than one
witness means it's true. *God-spell*:
the good news. First,
Matthew tells us a man's shriveled
hand was pulled taut. Another,
who couldn't see or hear,
was freed from demons.
A boy too looks to be dead
after Jesus's commands.
He tells the inquisitive men
to be the little children,
to cut off their feet, out
their eyes, away their tiny
hands. Then, Mark says as much.
And Luke. In no certain order.
But John sees none such storm.
Jesus loved him. John knows
the land. Jesus is reason
written and bowed
in the stars. He takes
His time. He is bread,
ripe fruit, both the shepherd
and the gate of the sheep.

The Lesser Water Boatman

Upside down he swims, showing
all of creation the wonder of body.

He turns his figure into a little boat:
back legs like oars fighting the still water.

He proves himself more and not less—
manhood whipping an earworm against his belly.

A true instrument. A harp, the throat,
rhythm sticks. He is both the gondola

and the love song. The scull itself
and the gondolier. Priapus

was the patron saint of sailors,
perhaps due to their years away

from shore. The seamen (lonely
and pained), the entire world around

them wet, carried wood in their pockets,
carved with the face of a lustful god.

Orgasm as Lapwing

The bird fakes hurt
to save herself. A moan
and bent limb, pretend
suffering to distract from her nest.
Even the peculiar way she takes
flight is something brutal
to behold: wingbeat slack
and unmeasured, then at once
a panicked and wounded bat.
Her pattern is both gentle
and drawn out as a river, an unhurried
bandit, and labored as a blacksmith.
The lapwing is rarely secretive.
Long-winded, she screams
a small murder as she flickers by.
This note is royal. High as the tuft
of down crowning the head
she has forgotten, the brain
full of worries violently
blown away.

Erection

My husband lets me look
at it for a while. A tight vein,
almost breaking. Perfect flower,
thick vine branch. I can taste it,
like a phantom limb, long after,
when my mouth is dry: salt
and flesh. Delicate thin skin.
Pink. Pink. A mimic
of what it wants—how hidden
like a young woman inside.
Cunning animals
trick their way in:
a reverse orchid, the prick
of a stitching spider, a katydid,
a mollusk, some flatworm
within the eye of a snail who sneaks
off to the belly of a songbird.
　　　　I trust its arrival
like tears, like vomit. The body
telling its secrets. The body
reaching. The body wanting
to be seen.
　　The body in love.

Valentine

You say a white-throated bird
has a call *like a navy whistle*;
I say the fur on the throat
of an elk is a *bell*. I say
there is a difference between
call and song: chip-up, an alarm,
thin cry, so happy. You say
sand that's hot enough turns
to glass. I say   the leaves
fell all day, and the dog
scooped them up like bars
of sunlight. I say the trees
are breathing for us. You say
the trees are the earth's lungs.

                    I say when you
see a bow, the sun is behind you.
I say it's in my book of stars.
You say   I say   you say

The Quickening

       Our yard is overtaken
by birds of prey. Hawks and kites
in the big tree—the one that pops
with fireflies like Christmas. I thought
we might make a garden this year,
but the ground keeps turning up
bolts without heads, strings looped
to pieces of plastic.
Where do the marbles and bottle caps
come from? They stamp bruises
in the shape of them on my feet.
I shudder at the idea of the origin
of birds. A visitation is a sight, a flutter
a delight. I call you in by the window
to watch them roost. *Come look!*
They leave before you get to see them.
They leave whenever they want.
To be quick is to be alive.

Wedding Night

Fuck like you're getting back
at God. Pull your long,
heavy white skirt over your head.

After you both finish, do the tricks
you heard girls talk about
in school: jump from the bed,

piss, and pray. Watch the doves alight
on the hotel balcony. Their coos mistaken
for owl sounds.

Elfland

When I woke, the little bird
in my belly had flown away.
My chest, a box of bees,
oddly still. We were shocked
to learn it was growing at all.
Just days after the wedding,
flowers in my hair like a May queen,
I was more than myself. Child from
a birdseed, a magic bean. Once upon a time,
our little house was broken into;
for hours, we didn't notice, until that chair
there was no longer, the drawer a mess,
the front window open just enough—*oh, I see*
—to let them slip away.

Nesting

What if our child
had been seven or eight? you said.
It could have been worse,
I admit. We could have
picked a name, painted a room,
replaced the blue with yellow.

I walked through the woods today
and noticed the canopy of trees,
thought *canopies on wagons, on beds.*
The third time at least, saw a doe and her fawn.

      For now, we will trim the front
walk, pay down our debts,
                chop down

    the dying dogwoods
from the lawn.

flying change

you showed me pegasus,
shaped like a crooked box,
and said that was his body.
there were other stars we couldn't see
that finished him: his head and legs,
the most beautiful parts of a dashing horse.
                 wings hidden in the dark sky.
the first two weeks of pregnancy are before
you've even had sex—near time traveling.
a person starts as just half of who they might become.
dream of our baby as a raspberry, a rapid evolution.
animal with tail and frog feet. the box jellyfish in final bell form.
or from old science textbooks, the little tiny horse the size
of a fox doubling and redoubling into the horses we now ride.
the mythic horse sprang from breaking waves, measures
sea, clay, and monster. a white horse, as wild
as his mother's serpentine hair, sinuous,
loose-limbed. from the state we're in,
the stars are starting to show again—
cold diamonds with crisp edges.
womb emptied my first birthday
as a married woman. we either look
our blessings in the mouth or run
breakneck toward a future.

Origin of God

Think of your parents before you.
First children themselves, fourth-graders
when Kennedy was shot. Half of you inside
your mother, even then. Months away
from a first confession.
                         Then meeting
by chance in a drive-in parking lot, your future
father mistaking your mother for some other
girl with long black hair. And with one child
of their own, a son. And a miscarriage
and uncertainty if they wanted to try
for you at all. Before people began, a story
opened with the heavens. But once before
that time, almost before time could be,
God spoke of Himself in plural. Said men
should *rule over* what they could never control.
His own snakes denning underground in winter,
a time of water. Snakes in a neighbor's tall grass
near your childhood home. Snakeskin
in the basement of your current one.
The heavens in pieces: stardust at night,
storm clouds by day. Think back further.
To your four grandparents. Each on various farms
in rural Kentucky. Now your great-grandparents,
ancestors—fruitful and multiplying backwards
until the numberless funnel back down to two.
And finally, just one.
And nothing. A zero, like an egg. Full of unknowns:
part of a son, a daughter, or a tangle of snakes inside
the body of a child.

Strawberry Moon

You were right.
The sky was haunting, so blue
it frightened me: the clouds purple
and black against more darkness.
The edge of the moon sharp
enough it keened. The heat ruthless
and hard. Rose moon, hot moon.
Last night you called me in
to witness the street lit up like high noon
through the bathroom window's glass blocks.
                              I don't have time
for this was how I put it. But by daybreak,
once in fifty years, and I missed it.

We begin another year together.
I throw empty threats into the air
at no one. Toss them up like glitter.
At your job, you are chased down
the street by a vicious dog, your arms
full of letters. Threatened by an old man
for junk mail. The world is relentless
in its work. Taxing. Ten years in
and no children. Weekends spent
patrolling for a new place to live.
You said now you could see three planets
all at once. *Jupiter. Saturn. Mars.*
There, there. And there. Index
finger exacting. The heat doesn't forgive.
Clean sheets pulled from the dryer
sparked in my hands. I was ready
for the night, but it was this morning.
The moon soaking in honey.

Honest Signals

The peacock roosts high.
He drops his feathers
like Rapunzel's shock of hair,
belly whirring with seed heads
and frogs. He wants to be seen.
Limned the color of deep water,
          it is his duty to display.
Most animals cannot fake strength.
They fight for the ordinary:
to breed and to eat. They use
what they have to get by.
A little brown bird
with the whitest crown
is tapped king. Antelopes
spring to prove lightsome,
that they can outrun
what comes for them.
A satin bowerbird makes
a blue room for his mate.
Decked with jewels, berries,
beads, money, glass, trash.
Bright things pretty as her eyes.
He pretends he is water, a man.

Reasons We Should Be Together

You let me paint your front door green.
I let you put your initials in me
like a tree or wet cement.
This evening we tried to pull
tall posts out of thick stone
in your front yard. My brother
said the best strategy was to wrap
chains around the wood and jerk-force
them out with our station wagon.
He once saw our cousin put his truck
in drive and rip the chain clear,
the metal braid horrific as a whip.

The Night We Decided Was a Day

On the drive back, a crow shreds a black snake.
I did a loop in the car just to watch it up close
again. But then, home, just like that: in the kitchen,
you stood laughing. Your brother and the radio.
Little boys silly over prank calls. This is the first night
my thinking moves brightly, a supernova.
You choose utopia. The ground bursts
with buttercups, the trees with apples
and pecans. *Come with me,* you sing. My mind
is a black bird, purple shine at the slightest shift:
everything basic is animal is holy.

Credits

Thank you to the editors of the journals in which the following poems first appeared:

"Thought Inventory with Rorschach and Caesura" appeared in *Ecotone*, no. 29, Spring 2020.

"The Miracle of the Pigs" appeared in *Cream City Review* 43, no. 2, Fall/Winter 2019.

"Animals in Captivity" appeared in *The Greensboro Review*, no. 106, Fall 2019.

"Mnemonics" appeared in *The Southern Review* 55, no. 2, Spring 2019.

"Orbs" appeared in *The Harvard Review*, no. 53, Spring 2019.

"Landscape Where I Forget My Father" appeared in *Phoebe* 48, no. 1, Winter 2019.

"Letting Go" was featured online on *The Spectacle*'s *REVUE*, 2019.

"Honest Signals" appeared in *North American Review* 304, no. 1, Winter 2019.

"Inscape" appeared in *The Gettysburg Review* 31, no. 3, Autumn 2018.

"Parable" appeared in *Prairie Schooner* 92, no. 3, Fall 2018, and was reprinted on *Verse Daily*.

"First Mirror" appeared in *FIELD*, no. 98, Spring 2018.

"Eschatology" appeared in *The Moth*, no. 34, Autumn 2018.

"Ode to the Cannibal" appeared on *Memorious*, no. 29, December 2018.

"The Meaning of God" and "Origin of God" appeared in *Image*, no. 98, 2018.

"The Men" appeared in *ZYZZYVA*, no. 113, Fall 2018, and was reprinted in *Best New Poets 2018*.

"The Lesser Water Boatman" appeared on *The Collagist*, no. 95, February 2018.

"What the Eclipse Does to Animals" appeared in *The Journal* 42, no. 2, Spring 2018.

"flying change" and "In the Myths" appeared in *Third Coast*, no. 46, 2018.

"Strawberry Moon" appeared in *AGNI* 86, 2017.

"Topography of a Bird" appeared in *Sugar House Review*, no. 15, Spring/Summer 2017.

"Kingdom" appeared in *Poetry Northwest*, Summer and Fall 2017.

"Original Meal" appeared in *Nasty Women Poets: An Unapologetic Anthology of Subversive Verse*, eds. Grace Bauer and Julie Kane (Sandpoint, ID: Lost Horse Press), September 6, 2017.

"Grandmothers" appeared in *Best New Poets 2016*.

"Hubris" appeared in *New South* 10, no. 2, 2017.

"A Figure for the Holy Ghost" appeared in *Hunger Mountain*, no. 21, 2017.

"The Godwit" and "Erection" appeared in *New American Writing*, no. 35, 2017.

"Landscape Where I Miss My Mother" appeared in *Poetry Ireland*, no. 122, 2017.

"The Screwworm" appeared in *Barrow Street*, Winter 2017/2018.

"Orgasm as Lapwing" and "Fear" appeared in *Alaska Quarterly Review* 34, no. 1/2, Summer/Fall 2017.

"The Night We Decided Was a Day" appeared in *Epoch* 66, no. 1, 2017.

"Song of the Cock" appeared on *Unsplendid* 6, no. 3, February 2017.

"Ruth" appeared in *Virginia Quarterly Review* 92, no. 2, Spring 2016.

"The Cow's Eye" appeared in *Oxford Poetry*, Winter 2016.

"Animals in the Bible" appeared in *The Hollins Critic* 53, no. 4, October 2016.

"Christ is a Great Blue Heron" appeared in *Spoon River Poetry Review* 41, no. 2, Winter 2016.

"Wilding" appeared in *The Laurel Review* 49, no. 2, 2016.

"The Godhead" appeared in *Sycamore Review* 27, no. 2, Winter/Spring 2016.

"Some Things Have Been Heard Enough" appeared in *Bat City Review*, no. 12, 2016.

"Grackles" appeared in *Bellingham Review*, no. 72, Spring 2016.

"Orrery" appeared in *Southern Humanities Review* 50, no. 1/2, 2016.

"First Death Ever Filmed" appeared in *PRISM* 53, no. 4, Summer 2015.

"The Country" appeared in *Poet Lore* 110, no. 1/2, 2015.

"The Leonids" appeared on *The Cortland Review*, no. 67, 2015.

"Double Star—" appeared in *Potomac Review*, no. 56, Spring 2015.

"Sacred Heart" was featured online on *The Pinch*, 2014.

"Frog Gig, 1983" appeared in *The Southeast Review* 31, no. 2, 2013.

"Reasons We Should Be Together" appeared in *Columbia Poetry Review*, no. 25, 2012.

"Animals" appeared in *Mississippi Review*, Winter 2011.

"Blindfold" appeared in *Mid-American Review* 30, no. 1/2, Fall 2009/ Spring 2010.

Notes

The book's epigraph is from the New King James Version of the Bible.

"Animals in the Bible" responds to a July 2015 article in the *Daily Mail* by Thomas Burrows entitled "A Pitiful End for the Animals of Georgia's Flooded Zoo."

"Ruth" was inspired by news stories from California and Atlantic City in 2014 and 2015 and Molly Menschel's documentary *Just Another Fish Story*, about a beached whale in Maine.

"The Meaning of God" references the King James Version of the Bible with "creeping things" (Genesis 7:23) and the New International Version of the Bible with "the vault of the sky" (Genesis 1:17).

Harry Wallop's September 2014 *Telegraph* article explains, "The customary way of eating ortolan, a delicate songbird, involves the diner covering his or her head with a large napkin. Tradition dictates that this is to shield—from God's eyes—the shame of such a decadent and disgraceful act." This is referred to in "Song of the Cock."

In "Original Meal," *mali* references the Vulgate translation of a word used in Genesis 2:17. There is confusion over the translation of *mălum* (Latin for "evil") versus *mālum* (Latin/Greek for "apple").

"Repletion" responds to an article that is actually titled "Men Catch Shark on North Carolina Beach as String of Attacks Rattle Nerves" [*sic*], by Emily Shapiro and Alana Abramson, via ABC News in July 2015.

"What the Eclipse Does to Animals" responds in part to an article by
Caroline Mortimer in the *Independent* in July 2017 entitled "Bull Kills
Itself after Horns Set on Fire at Spanish Fiesta."

"The Miracle of the Pigs" begins with a reference to a story in the *Daily
Mail* from August 2009 entitled "Scientists Baffled as 'Suicidal' Cows
Throw Themselves Off Cliff in Switzerland."

"Kingdom" partially references a September 2016 article in *New Scientist*
entitled "Five Wild Lionesses Grow a Mane and Start Acting Like
Males" [*sic*], by Karl Gruber.

"Hubris" references articles in the *Washington Post* from the spring and
summer of 2016. The actual phrasing used was "damaged masculinity."

"The Screwworm" partially references a CNN article by Susan Scutti
from October 2016 entitled "Florida Using 'Overwhelming Force' to
Fight Flesh-Eating Screwworms."

"Man, Beast, Lion, Bird" features an epigraph from Saint Thomas
Aquinas that is found in *Summa Theologica*, vol. 1.

"Orbs" features an epigraph from Martin Luther found in Roland
Bainton's *Erasmus of Christendom*.

The final three stanzas of "The Godwit" reference the trial of Kenneth
Parks in Ontario in 1987.

"Immolation" references a story about the pelican that may have
existed prior to Christianity. Father William P. Saunders explains the
intersection of allusions found in Dante's *Divine Comedy*, bestiaries,
Hamlet, and Aquinas's "Adoro te devote" in a letter on the *Arlington
Catholic Herald* online.

Born and raised in Kentucky, JENNIE MALBOEUF received a BA at Centre College and an MFA at the University of North Carolina at Greensboro. Her poems have appeared in *The Gettysburg Review, VQR, The Southern Review, Best New Poets,* and elsewhere. She teaches writing at Guilford College and lives in North Carolina with her husband, David, and dog, Mavis.